MR HENDRIX
AND THE TROUBLESOME TENNESSEE TOPPER

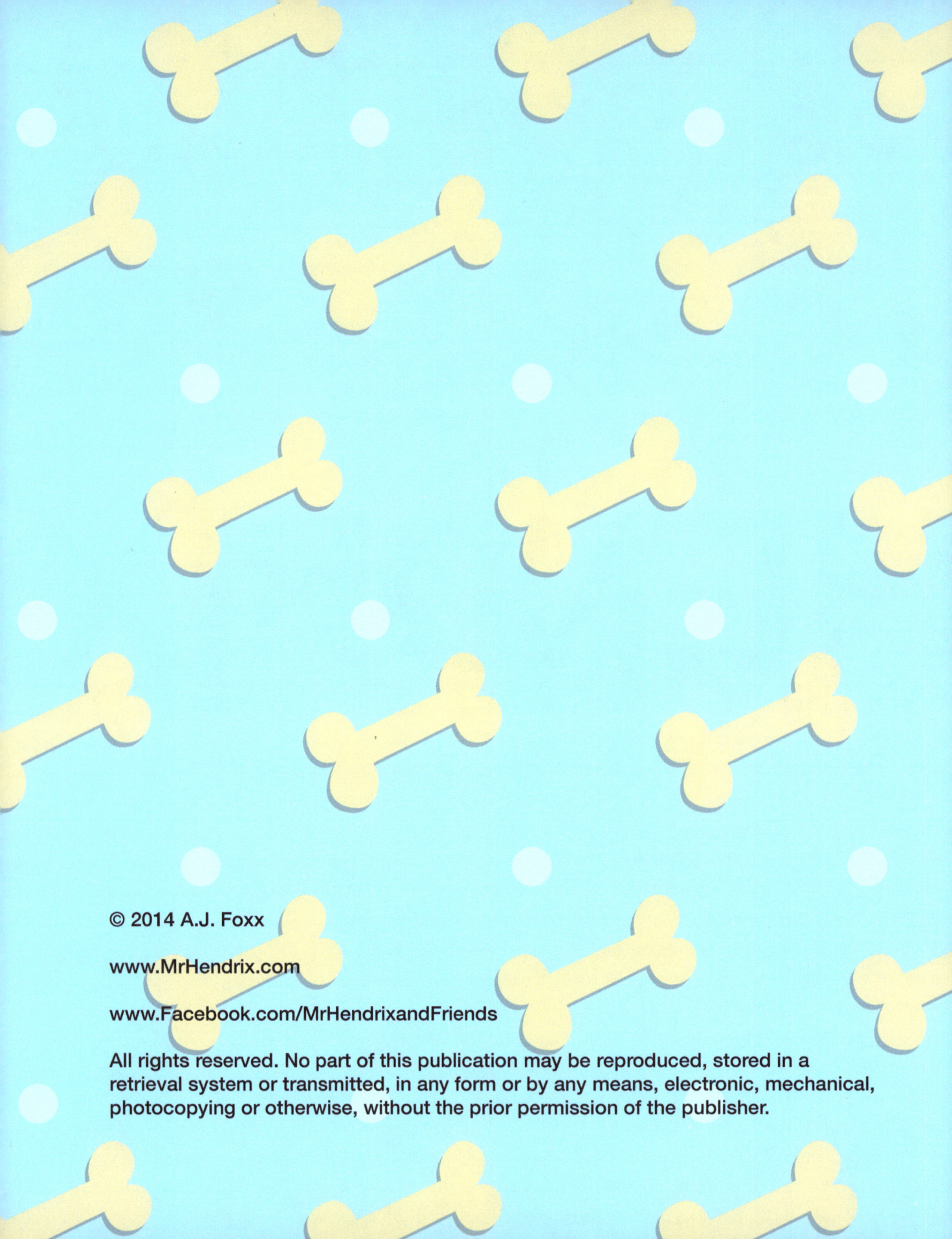

© 2014 A.J. Foxx

www.MrHendrix.com

www.Facebook.com/MrHendrixandFriends

All rights reserved. No part of this publication may be reproduced, stored in a retrieval system or transmitted, in any form or by any means, electronic, mechanical, photocopying or otherwise, without the prior permission of the publisher.

It's a beautiful warm and sunny day.
Olivia is busy gardening, listening to her music.
Mr Hendrix, Kitty and Sid are playing in the garden.
Mr Hendrix is digging a very big hole,
while Kitty is carefully collecting flowers that have fallen from the trees.
Sid is slithering and sliding through the long grass.

Mr Hendrix is covered in soil from top to tail.
He shakes his head and starts a silly dance to get the soil off him.
Kitty and Sid start giggling.
"Oh 'endrix," says Kitty. "You are so funny."
Mr Hendrix keeps on dancing making them laugh and laugh.

Mr Hendrix sees all of the flowers in Kitty's paws.
"How many flowers have you collected Kitty?" asks Mr Hendrix.
Kitty and Sid start to count the flowers together.
"ONE, TWO, THREE, FOUR, FIVE."
"Oh 'endrix, they are so beautiful." says Kitty.
"I have two red, one yellow, one orange and one purple".

Mr Hendrix, Kitty and Sid carry the flowers over to their den at the back of the garden.
The den is hidden away behind a huge yellow rose bush where Harry the Hippy Dippy Hedgehog is keeping guard.
Inside, the den is full of treasures they have all collected:
a red rug, a magical book, a string of pearls,
gold coins and special treats.
Kitty begins to decorate the den with her pretty flowers.
They hear the doorbell ring. Mr Hendrix is excited because his brother is coming to visit.
Kitty is nervous. She has heard that Mr Hendrix's brother can be a little bit mischievous.

Dressed in a top hat, bow tie and swinging a silver cane, Mr Hendrix's brother swaggers through the house and into the garden to greet them all, puffing out his chest proudly.
He wears a shiny black eye with pride following a fight with a ferret.
'Good morning beautiful," he says bending down to kiss Kitty's paw.
'My name is Tennessee Topper," he winks.
'Pleased to meet you," says Kitty shyly.

Tennessee Topper smiles, then turns to greet Mr Hendrix, placing his cane on Sid's tail to make him squirm.
"Ooooowwwwww!" squeals Sid. His eyes go as big as saucers.
"Don't do that to Sid, he's my friend," says Mr Hendrix crossly.
"Oh sorry, I didn't see you down there."
Tennessee Topper sniggers while strolling over to Kitty.

Tennessee Topper tells Kitty about his home.
"It's a charming castle in the country
with 10 bedrooms and a glorious, grand ballroom.
It's a magical kingdom and I am the King who prowls my land at night."
Kitty is in awe of Tennessee Topper.
Hendrix checks on Sid and warns of his brother's naughty ways.
"Well, do show me around my darling Kitty," says Tennessee
Topper, as he puts his paw around Kitty.
Kitty doesn't feel him steal her beautiful diamanté necklace.

Kitty happily shows Tennessee Topper around the garden.
"Look at all the flowers, they are so pretty," purrs Kitty.
"I suppose so," yawns Tennessee Topper.
They see a baby bird pecking in the soil.
Tennessee Topper marches over and kicks soil over the little bird making her cough and splutter.
"Stop it, don't be so cruel!" shouts Kitty.
Tennessee Topper chuckles to himself with a wide, wicked smile.
He swings his cane and knocks the heads off all the flowers.
Kitty feels sad.

"I'm sorry 'endrix but I don't like your brother, he is not a very nice dog at all," says Kitty.
She notices Mr Hendrix staring at her.
"Where is your beautiful sparkling collar?"
Kitty puts her paw to her neck.
'Oh no! I must have lost it," she cries.

"Maybe not Kitty."
He marches over to Tennessee Topper. "OK, hand it over," shouts Mr Hendrix.
"Whatever are you talking about?" replies a grinning Tennessee Topper.
"Kitty's diamanté collar, I know you have stolen it," Mr Hendrix barks angrily.
Harry the Hippy Dippy Hedgehog hears the quarrel and scurries over. "Hey guys, let's all calm down."

"Oh, dear boy, keep out of this," laughs Tennessee Topper as he kicks Harry up in the air.
Mr Hendrix, Kitty and Sid all look on in horror.
As Harry is kicked across the garden he leaves three sharp spikes in Tennessee Topper's paw.

Tennessee Topper suddenly shrieks out in pain and falls to the ground.
Kitty's beautiful diamanté necklace spills out of his pocket in front of Mr Hendrix.
Tennessee Topper looks angry that he has been caught.

Kitty and Sid gasp, they are shocked and upset.
Mr Hendrix picks up the beautiful necklace and places it around Kitty's neck.
"Oh Kitty, I am so very sorry," says Mr Hendrix.
"Don't be sorry, it's not your fault. Oh 'endrix you are my 'ero!" purrs Kitty.

Mr Hendrix, Kitty and Sid race over to Harry the Hippy Dippy Hedgehog.
Harry has wrapped himself in a little ball.
"Harry, Harry, are you OK?" asks Mr Hendrix.
Harry snuffles and huffles. "Yes I'm fine," he snorts.
"You are very brave," says Mr Hendrix, helping Harry back on his feet.
The hedgehog smiles then looks over to Tennessee Topper.
"But Hendrix, what are we going to do about your brother?"

Tennessee Topper is on the floor crying out in pain.
Mr Hendrix walks over to him and pulls the three spikes out of his paw.
"Thank you my dear brother," he says gratefully.
"Tennessee Topper, we should never steal from or hurt other people.
NEVER EVER," barks Mr Hendrix.
Tennessee Topper seems sorry and promises to be kind to Mr Hendrix
and his friends when he next comes to visit.
But only time will tell………

MR HENDRIX

Can you colour in this picture for Mr Hendrix?

MR HENDRIX

Can you colour in this picture for Mr Hendrix?

MR HENDRIX

Can you help Mr Hendrix spot the difference?

MR HENDRIX

There are six differences to spot

www.ingramcontent.com/pod-product-compliance
Lightning Source LLC
Chambersburg PA
CBHW041234040426
42444CB00002B/156